Ghost Voices

Ghost Voices

A POEM IN PRAYER

Quincy Troupe

TriQuarterly Books/Northwestern University Press
Evanston, Illinois

TriQuarterly Books
Northwestern University Press
www.nupress.northwestern.edu

Sections of *Ghost Voices*, in earlier and altered forms, have
appeared in *The Asian American Literary Review, Mission at Tenth,
Killens Review of Arts & Letters,* and *Konch Magazine.*

Printed in the United States of America

10   9   8   7   6   5   4   3   2   1

Library of Congress Cataloging-in-Publication Data

Names: Troupe, Quincy, author.
Title: Ghost voices : a poem in prayer / Quincy Troupe.
Description: Evanston, Illinois : TriQuarterly Books/
    Northwestern University Press, 2019.
Identifiers: LCCN 2018028675 | ISBN 9780810138995
    (pbk. : alk. paper) | ISBN 9780810139008 (ebook)
Subjects: LCSH: Slave trade—Africa, West—Poetry. | Slave trade—
    America—Poetry. | African diaspora—Poetry.
Classification: LCC PS3570.R63 G46 2019 | DDC 811/.54—dc23
LC record available at https://lccn.loc.gov/2018028675

For Oliver Lee Jackson, Mildred Howard,
Allison Hedge Coke, Margaret Porter Troupe,
and to the memory of my mother,
Dorothy Smith Marshall

Contents

Ghost Voices

Chorus Song:
Crossing Big Salt Water

we are crossing,
we are
crossing,
we are crossing in big salt water,

we are crossing,

crossing under a sky of no guilt
we have left home

though we know we will go back
someday,
see our people
as we knew them,

we have left
everything behind,
we seek somewhere,
our dreams somewhere,

our dreams out there,
somewhere

we are searching,
we look everywhere
seeking *IT*,
we are seeking *IT*

we don't know where,
but we are going,
we are going, seeking,
looking for *IT* everywhere

we are crossing,
crossing in big salt water,
we are under the waves,
the ships and enslaved,

they survived our deaths
but found their own
became slaves crossing in the storms

packed,
packed into stinking holds,

we are crossing over as spirits beneath
those up there
up on ships,
packed in their own stink
inking dark holes,
packed in their gored,
exfoliated flesh,
eviscerated, we are still here underneath
riding the backs of african ghost crabs
underneath the big salt water
under a sky with no guilt,

we are crossing,
we are crossing over together
over and under,
we are crossing

spirits down here,
flesh packed up there,

in them stinking ships
packed with our flesh

another death
sharks strung out for miles
behind the ships,
we are crossing,
we are crossing,

riding the backs of african ghost crabs

we are crossing,
we are crossing in big salt water,

we are going somewhere,
where we will find our kinfolks,
somewhere,

we left our homes,
but we carry it with us
where we are going,
after crossing
we will fly back home,
speak through the shadows,
we will not be strangers
when we will seek *IT*
we will find our *FREEDOM*,

we are crossing,
we are
crossing,
we are crossing in big salt water

First Take

from my terrace in goyave, guadeloupe,
eye listen,
hear sea waves washing in whispering lullabies
combing through sand with raspy voices,
licking with lapping finger tongues
over a script lost
and secret coded utterances sigh,

eye am hearing
wailing journeys crawling across time,
crawling onshore
here in guadeloupe,

     this volcanic butterfly island
     rising
from the dark howling bottom
where translucent spirits
cover their black holes for eyes,
diffuse their hands,
speak through silence,

what they saw blew out
the lights of their sights
     400 years back
listen now,
hear them speak
lost rhythms
scripted in the skins of talking drums,
hear them speak,
hear the wailing,

caterwauling language spoken
through pulsating glissandos

eye hear them
throbbing, calling in my dreams

you hear them calling too,
you hear them,
with their caterwauling voices
speaking directly in our chambers
speaking directly to you

Arrival of Ghost Voices

in the dead of night
ghost voices come,
surround me
in sleep,

hold nothing
back from the cocked ears of slumber,
sharp as the blade of a knife
paring sweetness
when slicing through
the blush of a mango's skin reveals
what the palate and memory evoke,

those voices
with their severed tongues
castrated from *FREEDOM*
now carry the cruel
passage of pitched voices
hoarse from the salt water
crossing, now
voices wailing with pain
while being eaten with teeth of ghost hyenas,
glowing like skin of translucent piranhas
still searching for flesh somewhere,

now my dreams are a fever

filled with sacred chants and dancing priests,
red-eyed witch doctors
who know secrets
howled from the underworld of death,

they will serve this potion of
a voodoo white flower
to the disbelievers,
turn them into zombies

eye hear the arrival of those
raised holy voices, hear them,
see them in my imagination
riding backs of african ghost spirit crabs
as they arrive
here in my dreams,
eye am listening,
hearing their siren calls
eye am listening

prayer seducing in the night,
eye am listening, hearing your spirit
voices rising from the sea surrounding
the wings of a beautiful butterfly
shaped like this island,
this place where ancestors are kept,

voices in whirlpools eddying
flowing on shores curled like lovers,

their love raptures whispering,
riffing in my heart,

eye hear some of them
howling through the crossing

inside polished bones with their
wind and tongues beseeching

those who survived,
in the newborn america,
scaffolded from within

words from skin-wombs of talking drums
they came through the door of no return

the reaper took them down
to swim inside battalions
sweeping west,
just below the terrace
where *eye* am lost in dreaming

                    eye listen, listen closely now too

the skin of the drums
flying on wings of tongues
washed ashore seeking redemption,
sulfur whispers, winding themselves
around faith like an octopus with gold tentacles
inside rivers of blood-fingers,

like birds on the wind
there is a rhythm
there, where death even has a rhythm
when sharks guillotine the necks of kinfolks,
hear them screaming in salt water

listen now to the caterwauling history
in the scaffolding litany of sacred voices,
beseeching sea waves of gospels,
listen to the voices swirling out of
these watery litanies foaming,
hear what they say, listen,
listen closely to what they say

IV

Transferring the Dreams
of the Ghost Voices

& so each day the sun rises,
voices resurrect
the morning mist of memory
we will all be reborn one day

these fevered dreams
anchored in history,
why these voices flew
like birds in springtime,
they took us there

because we only knew

to keep on going,
seeking *IT* we knew
to keep on going
seeking *IT*

V

The New Dream
of Ghost Voices

where does breath go after flesh falls away from bone,
does it remember

perhaps it's there
tangled in the fog
of our willful erasure

where does breath go when we disrobing history
plunder the gold coin chests of enslaving
callous men loving mammon,
blinded by evil, the earth now a furnace,

can we still be reborn

beyond structure,
tongues re-creating themselves,
changing, fusing inside poetry,
rhythms evoked by drum masters'
onomatopoeia, cracking
shrapnel flying inside words,
the moon rising from its dark grave
above the promise death kept,
voices of redemption
within healing songs of light.
raising voices of redemption
above the promise death kept

VI

Chorus:
African Ghost Spirit Crabs
Cross Karukera
(Guadeloupe)

we arrived on this butterfly island
became birds flying in the mist of trees,
crabs crawling sideways

we, the shadows, flocks of flying ghost voices
moved across slowly, sometimes quickly
through places where a few people with skins white
as the moon
glowed in starlight

many look the way we look
when we were alive with skin—
except we had skins black as midnight—
diamond eyes set deep in midnight skins
soft as the love of our mothers—

others carried cold eye of snakes—
chained, their eyes sad,
heads hung low as beaten dogs,
as birds lying on earth with broken wings

some of us decided to stay
the beauty of the place,
others decided *FREEDOM* was somewhere else,
and went on looking for *IT*,
where,
we didn't know where,
but we knew *IT* wasn't here,
was out there somewhere,

so we left in the mist
moving from tree to tree,
gathered in open meadows,
some crawled sideways,
others made their way flying,
we didn't know where,
but we knew we were going,
moving toward somewhere, looking for *IT*
out there somewhere
though we didn't know where,
but we were going, seeking *IT*,

we came upon another big salt water,
beneath the gray sky of no remorse,
towering waves full of savage,
unhinged, leering skeletons,

still we crawled sideways toward some

where, we didn't know where,
but we were still looking for *IT*,
though we didn't know where *IT* was
but it was there in our imaginations,
so we moved forward toward *IT*,

we came to be reborn

VII

Transition: Guadeloupe (Karukera) to the Gulf of Mexico

ghost voices left the north shores
of the butterfly island,
rode crests of curling waves,
followed ships crossing the caribbean
blown north, rode wings of birds,
backs of dolphins,
vortexes of hurricane winds,
waves of howling demons, lashings
with god's breath

whiplashed voices of the enslaved
chained to ships docking
in the dominican republic, haiti, here

the spirit of an old black man: legba
sitting, holding a small corn pipe drooping
from his protruding, castanet lips
clapping out biographical information
when the spirits ask him who he was,
he tells them he is the god
who controls the crossing over
from one world to the other,

tells them he holds the keys,
tells them he can make a way
for them to find *IT*
only if they listen.

legba speaks like the wise old men
they came from
deep down in their memories,

they recognize his ancient spirit,
they ask legba what they have to do to find *IT*,

then a woman named erzulie,
wearing three rings on three fingers for three husbands
who worship her named agwe, damballah & ogun
appears like an apparition from the bushes,
legba tells them she is the voodoo goddess of beauty,
                                    love, all things human,
her first husband agwe is sovereign of the seas,
the other two are loas, spirits, like african ghost crabs,

then legba brings them together
with a wave of his hands, his fire-
red eyes rolling upwards, as his head shakes
strange words spill from his slapping
protruding castanet lips, foam dripping
from both corners of his mouth
like strings of tiny pearls
as he anoints them part crab, part loa,
he directs them with a wave of his hands
& a command from his voice
full of clapping bones
to go forward toward the big salt water,
he hands them the gift of transparency
so they can travel unseen seeking the promise,
they are told to follow black birds,
pass jamaica, cuba,
to enter the gulf,

search for *IT*—*FREEDOM,* then
the hoodoo spirit crabs slip into the warm salt
waves pulling them west as the black birds fly
like periods ending sentences

Song of the Hoodoo
Spirit Crabs

we are crossing another big salt water,
we are moving, going forward
after shedding our old selves, we have new pincer claws,
we crawl sideways, backwards, go forward,
sometimes we can lift up from the bottom of the sea,
swim on top, maybe later we will fly—some of us
already do as mist—like birds, but now we are crawling west,
northwest, following black birds,
where we don't know where, but we are going
searching for where we think *IT* is,
                          going where we think the promise is,
we are going forward with memories of the old
                              mixed with the new, now

transparent we are looking to find another way, a third way,
leading us into the future
where we will find *IT*/the promise,
                          where, we don't know where
but we are going,
where, we don't know where

but we do know *IT* is out there, somewhere,
& we will find it, we need to be reborn, again,

again & again, we need to be reborn again

IX

The New World: Moving North

hoodoo crab spirits followed
where slave vessels took them,
they followed these wretched ships carrying their kinfolks,
packed like sardines crossing the gulf,
wasting away in these rocking & rolling wretched vessels,
some leap overboard,
dangling chains from their bodies,

the eye of the sun & moon bless them,

watched them go under, sink to the bottom of the sea,
where they became ghost voices,
the long procession
following the ships,
joined translucent hoodoo spirit crabs
following these ships, who had once shared
         the same skin color as black birds, crows,

hoodoo spirit crabs began howling—spirituals
in a silence deep inside themselves

they saw black birds—flying over the gulf,
a narrow slit of earth—an open mouth,
shaped like a vagina?
carved into the head of a body of land
sprawling northward, was it a woman?—
where a snaking tributary flowed south,
         emptied out into the gulf,
a snaking figure of water
later called the mississippi

many hoodoo crabs
.voked mystery, magic
here in the king of zulus, marching funeral bands
sweating music on streets of new orleans,
                              practicing voodoo of legba, erzulie, agwe,

others felt *IT* wasn't abundant enough here, so
kept moving north through silt, mud covering graves
down deep in the mississippi river bottom, spirit bloods
crawling sideways toward where, they didn't know

where, sometimes hooking their spirits
                      onto underbellies of ships,

heading north now over, underwater beneath skies
where black birds—crows—fly,
the spirits loved the color of these birds
because it was once the shade of their skin before they became
hoodoo spirit crabs

african ghost spirit crabs
crossing the atlantic, caribbean, then the gulf
before entering this snaking muddy river—
before time draped a cape of twilight when the one-eyed cyclop
peeked down posing as the moon, before night spread
its immense winged garment of darkness across the sky's black
expanse, deep, brilliant with stars embedded
                              like millions of jeweled diamonds,

spread out on a jeweler's black cloth,

when wolves howled everywhere
hoodoo spirit crabs kept moving north as crows fly,
towards where they didn't know where,
crawling sideways

hoodoo spirit crabs found spaces in the blues,
would be born in the womb of the delta,
where the rivers
tallahatchie, yalobusha would marry,
hold lynched bodies, now bones of kinfolks,
become the yazoo river, where cotton would be king,

hoodoo crabs kept moving north as crows fly,
spirits searching
though no one still knew where *IT* was
they crawled sideways back into the mississippi

made their way again through mud, silt & bones
northward, to where they don't know where,
but following the flight of crows they came to
where memphis would grow up,
raise up beale street—barbecue,
the blues

some hoodoo crabs found home
in memphis, rooted their spirits deep in that soil,
nothing would ever be the same again—everything changed
here in this evolving space of brutality

X

Going Back to Goyave, Guadeloupe: What My Ears Needed to Hear

now *eye* want to hear hoodoo crabs speak
onomatopoeia language macking, expanding
without a trace of boundaries,
eye want to hold nothing back reaching for *IT*,

eye want to kill muted voices murmuring in silence,
because of severed tongues held up high on bloody sticks,
heads on poles

eye know flowers will bloom
wondrous colors somewhere after the moon has been
swallowed by rising sunlight, then *eye* want to hear
voices swelling, filling up hours with dazzling beauty,
                                        firing my imagination with dreams,
now *eye* need light, see hints of sunbeams blooming,
becoming daylight spreading, hints of rapture,
underwater, where desiccated
african ghost crabs crawled sideways
through atlantic bottom silt, over bones, rocks, where
leering skeletons peeked out of lost ships, *eye* want to hear
anthropomorphic
sidewinding music across holy
floors of the caribbean sea, the gulf of mexico,
the big muddy mississippi, traveling incognito
besides bug-eyed catfish, speaking through invisible
tongues of wind saying—though this might not be true—

we have arrived in this space after a lifetime
crossing, from the east side of the big salt waves,
came dragging chains shackling our bony bodies

osent flesh, our terrible, long passage
metamorphosing us into spirits, tonguing breath,
voices full of mystery, songs, religious utterances,
amulets, tribal practices, accents anchored inside blood,
threading through languages no one here understood,
but we have brought them—these foreign things—here
across foaming salt waters to extend in prayer
our translucent hands seeking joy, love,

                              searching for *IT* religiously,

eye hear voices stained with pillaged histories
bloody with pain—beauty too—bringing magic,
music, joy here too, telling me their stories,
revealing themselves as truth carriers,
sweet manna coursing through their narratives
with octopus tentacles wrapping around to hold them
as they swirl through my life, they are whirling dervishes
riding inside these crab spirit-voices, swimming there
alongside fish, they have gathered seeds, rooted them
within their essence, secrets, cross-fertilizing lineages,
shared with miracles holding them—me—one
to another, anchored here within
the confidential privilege of knowing
the sweet song still sings in them, surging through
their symphonies, blood, knowing lullabies whisper still
inside wind music, breathing, pulsating through trees
each day the sun rises, ghost voices washing ashore
in foaming raucous waves of the atlantic, combing
over rocks, sand, carrying primordial history

to me here, now, bringing a constant reminder
filled with deep wonder—

we have come to this butterfly island
with our whispering voices intact,
hear these voices full of prayer
foaming & whispering onshore every day

& *eye* hear their unleashed whisperings now
as prayer after locks of history were broken,

                              eye understand
ghost voices housed inside crabs
who moving slowly, resolutely
crossing over atlantic bottoms for centuries,
having dragged themselves here, wailing sacred
utterances, carrying amulets, fragments, re-creating old practices,
accents binding, anchoring within blood, song,

rolling now, rising up, spraying riddles, caterwauling,
emanating hoarsely
climbing toward the surface of salt water, river water,
symphonic voices roaring old secrets,
swept here through battalions of foaming waves,
swept west carrying enigmas, secret practices—

can't you hear us howling to your hearts now,
we african ghost crab spirit wailers,
metamorphosed into hoodoo crabs,
who once rode the backs of bucking dolphins
don't you recognize us rolling in snarling memories
washing onto shores of guadeloupe in foaming waves

ow, in wave after wave speaking of forgotten bones,
speaking now in unknown rhythmic tongues,
trooping forward now in wave after wave,
rumbling toward the unknown world in the west,
can't you hear us now speaking to you
with hoarse voices howling like wolves, demons,
can't you hear us howling this hoarse truth

XI

Hoodoo Crab Spirits Find New Homes

across the caribbean,
up & down the mississippi river,
the past turning on a dime,
who surviving the middle passage
now are howling sacred memories

in hoodoo spirit crabs,
who are creators of a new language
threading through their music, poetry, dance,
new hoodoo,
speaking through me, now,
woven inside dreams, blackamoors speaking,
transforming voices breathing in america now,

hear a new language forming in the sound of a baby
eagle's voice,
hear voices of honey being made
when hummingbird wings blur music of bees
as an act of faith, breath, a love
processing poetry heard under sunrays knifing
through shadows as filigreeing light speckling
beyond even megadeaths, life blooming
under umbrella canopies of trees, where death was heard
under them in the old country rattling breaths of gazelles
after their throats were caught in vise-gripping jaws
of cheetahs, lions, leopards, all over africa,
the words here in this poem imagine the terror
breathing through that memory
stirring in ancestors, before silt settled over
their entombed bodies, before flesh fell away from bones,

turned to stone on the bottom of the atlantic,
the caribbean sea, countless river bottoms, lakes here,
birthing "strange fruit" hanging from magnolia trees,
haunting later in lady day's voice,
under summer's green, or autumn's browning leaves,
before they started fluttering down like dead bees
when landscapes began turning white as frozen time,
when lungs gasped for air in sealed tombs of winter,

there are moments we can look up, see open skies,
imagination spreading over a meadow,
a space to step into a dream, lead us to ponder where
we have come from—a terrible journey filled with death
deep in the dark atlantic salt water—

now we might recognize *IT—FREEDOM*

winging up into the sky, flying (soaring) all the way
back home to africa, in our hearts & minds is as an act
of discovery, then flying back to this new place again
once we looked into the memory, heard
the rhythms up inside the tone of the old words—
forgotten for so long—& knew what
we had to know in that moment of recognition
our language is launched from here now
despite the terror of this new barbarous world

XII

Surviving

surviving in us here
are secrets, locking us one to another,
vowels roll off tongues in rhythms
is what courses through blood, bone deep
in the marrow of identity sharing culture is voice,
fused inside fingers playing harmony on pianos,
melody in certain songs ears know, recognize
in hearts as a certain truth, as is the hand-built
scaffolding of architecture in language
lacing through lines of poetry, everyday speech,
evoked in guitars, harmonicas, a sense of recognition,
something ears can pass on to hearts,
through the sound of saxophones, trumpets
to brains, echoing familiarity, foreign, or local
idioms anchored in geographic places
as seeds blooming in spaces the ways people speak,
grow together, sharing ethos, values—
twin tuning forks serving as harmony,
locking into what eyes translate to hearts, brains,
dreams, visuals, outlines of faces, the shapes of eyes,
round with surprise, or oval with joy,
soft as flower petals—the breath of lips,
open, or closed, fires the imagination
to feel desire, kiss pillowing softness, licking,
engaging the tongue, sucking the fire passion
lying dormant in someone's heart,
pulled inside seduction of open lips
revealing pearls of white teeth, perfect
in their symmetry, beauty, as is

the resonant grace of a woman's face,
feline elegant stride, traces an antelope's
undulating rhythm in the sway of her hips,
is what signals hearts to beat wildly
for what is being promised here
in this moment, is delirious fervor,
is remembrance, emanating from deep
inside cultural transferal, a secret,
knowable through rhythms music creates,
shoots arrows into hearts,
as brains comprehend hearing time
beating as hearts, thumping as one
in a bass line unifying the pulsating music
fused inside a knowable feeling—is mystery
only disciples, initiates know the code to,
is the miracle glue holding culture together
inside memory, is what readers' ears
recognize in language of poetry,
is what rings the bell of shared identity

XIII

The Enlightened Awakening

Should God die, I would die.

——AKAN PROVERB

eye am back here in the dream of harlem
some call—mistakenly—"the hood,"
writing, creating neolistic forms of hybrid poetry,
though familiar in the echoing beat sluicing
through the musical structure of language,
after listening to ocean waves whispering
african history crossing the atlantic, the caribbean sea
on waves foaming onshore in goyave, guadeloupe,
having listened to those ancient voices,
those ancient forms telling me *eye* am old
but new here in this evolving place called
america, where new forms have been created—
work songs, spirituals, gospels, sermons, blues,
swing, jazz, rhythm 'n' blues, pop, rock, fusion, rap—
eye have come to follow creation down a path
attempting to raise up a new form with music in poetry
eye named seven-elevens, after the throw of the dice,
because seven throw eleven wins
in the game of dice, seven throw eleven wins *FREEDOM, IT,*
so *eye* began reaching back my fingers through words
to touch your spirit of new paths inside the beating
hearts of ancestors in this new world—duke ellington,
son house, muddy waters, howlin' wolf, screamin' jay hawkins,
bessie smith, ma rainey, miles davis, james brown, john coltrane,
michael jackson, sister rosetta tharpe, prince, otis redding,
curtis mayfield, sarah vaughan, jimi hendrix, mahalia jackson,
ray charles, ella fitzgerald, lloyd price, thelonious monk
& one still alive, around, singing today, aretha franklin—
in this moment reclaiming reconciliation, joy,

celebrating the obliterating journey of the middle passage
                              crossing, when every indicator informed us
all was lost in the bones dissolving into silt in that crossing,

but now *eye* know ancestors flew back spiritually
to the homeland, then winged forward through time
into the present, here—the future too—
                              as caressing spirits seduced me
through love as *eye* slept dreaming, in goyave, guadeloupe,
in the wee hours after midnight, ghost voices came to serenade
me inside my memories, brought their alchemy, rooted it there
inside my blood-gene chromosomes, where miracles can anchor
sacred secrets inside mystery, magic, can rise here privileged
in this confidential moment,

                              so *eye* felt your ancient spirit
again fusing with mine through space, across time—
through the distortion of words, languages,
                              syllables, sounds,
our tongues sluicing together now, forming a connective
tissue, infusing our languages rooted here in blood,
no matter we had become strangers, again—
as happened back then before the crossing
when tribalism, greed,

                              the lust for power
severed our connection from one another—
was the reason our ancestors were thrown to sharks,
the horrible bloodletting passage through waters of the atlantic,
while yours, dear ancestors, stayed there where you were,

lived through other forms of bloodletting,
enslavement, in the space you banished me from

now *eye* am telling you here you are forgiven
in this poem—now you must forgive yourself too & love
this stranger—brother, myself, a blackamoor—before you now,
because your blood-gene chromosome is linked to mine
in the form of a rod-shaped arm extending a handshake
across time, space, embracing us ancient spirit,
here in this poem, *eye* give to you now
                         this provenance of unconditional love,
take it, embrace it—me—now, grasp my hand
extended here, in this moment of reconciliation,
receive my invitation, dear spirit,
                                         brother, sister,
mother, father, uncle, aunt, cousin, blood,

accept my love, forgiveness, now, recognize
this new language coursing through my poem,
speaking for us now, here in this strange new place
in my voice infused with yours,
speaking in shared blood, scaffolded in shared horror
inflicted on us both—my dreaming thrown down linked now
through yours wallowing in guilt for casting me out—
knowing these crimes will be redressed inside
reconciliation, knowing our metamorphosis is a gift,
                         a metaphor leading to sacred love,
so *eye* extend to you now through this poem, brother,
sister, blood, knowing recompenses of this journey will be shared
as we move together into a future with our voices—

not theirs, not voices of our slavers—but ours
                    writing histories of our own blood shed
throughout the length of this passage,
knowing we are re-creating new history now—call it myth,
call it whatever, but it is our remembrance—
                    with our imaginations flying
as a breathing, living testimony, we are creating, evoking now
here in a living language full of new metaphors
                    sluicing off our own tongues
in the musical jambalaya we are speaking now
in this poem, breaking multilayered rhythms,
filled with neologisms, the model we stand with here,
reborn, secure in this voice we are speaking now—
reader, listener—our multilingual poetic voices
deep in new world vocabularies

                    galvanizing power in our invented forms
here, now on display in the creative forces we move through
as blackamoors, into an unknown future, we renew
our fecund imagination impregnating the language
found in our voices, we are breaking through linguistic paralysis,
raising up magic, mystery in this moment,
                    with poets creating new poetic forms,

seven throw eleven wins
the game of dice, seven throw eleven wins,

free of terror we are here
reborn, we breathe in the moment creating,
speaking the future in song

unafraid of madness of the past, we are
syncopating duke's magic,
the train whistle rambunctiousness in basie's
inventive, driving music,

the voodoo laced trumpet voice of shango riffs
nailing satchmo's gumbo voice,
the kansas city rooster sound of bird's hot
pepper soaring solo horn,
shooting white girl nodding sickness through his veins,
a sign of the times to come,
speaking through bud powell's catatonic words,
though one can see in his eyes
genius, slant of notes, riffs run off blurring wings
of his hummingbird fingers
flying over piano keys, tickling chords,

seven throw eleven wins
the game of dice, seven throw eleven wins

high priest of hipness monk, block
chording mysterioso's black & white keys,
shuffling his feet back & forth
under the piano, the fleet, high-flying
rat-tat-tat speedo brash licks
dizzy blows spitting bebop, with a cuban
flash up in his attitude

the president of hipness wearing a badge
saying *ividivi* sweet

jammin' soul bending syllables, blown wailing
through saxophone speak, bop cool
as the prince of darkness styled too hip for clues
to express through metaphors,
so he whispers muted kind of blue trumpet
licks creating new language
in music five times—so-called cool jazz, roadhouse
funk, rock 'n' roll, bitches brew,
on the corner—with those hip deep bass, drum grooves,

seven throw eleven wins
the game of life, seven throw eleven wins

leontyne price, black diva
from mississippi, soaring sonic hoodoo
voice breaking through barriers,
bringing erzulie to bach, beethoven, sounds
ella scats way way down deep
neologic word plays, ignoring dull ways
to phrase hoary song lyrics,

new takes on black spinning vinyl, lady day,
sarah, dinah, abbey, bold
carmen slick styling mcrae, cold-blooded vamp,
no-nonsense nina simone
dropping spells on those who heard her voice phrasing
deep mysterious élan,
oral language word playing in blues poets,
son house, muddy waters, bold
hoochie-coochie tumbling forty days, forty

nights stroking smokestack lightnin',
got my mojo workin', 'cause my love strikes quick,

seven throw eleven wins
the game of dice, seven throw eleven wins

cold lightning, howlin' wolf's songs,
mr. highway man at your back door moanin'
for his baby, a spoonful
of evil going down slow, built for comfort out
on the killin' floor, night
crawlin' king snake wang dang doodling, boogying
chuck berry's song, maybelline

pulsing in the wee wee hours thirty days,
you can't catch me, roll over
beethoven tell tchaikovsky the news, there's this
new music we call rhythm
& blues, cause there's too much monkey
bizness reelin' and rockin',
little queenie, my ding-a-ling, my own bizness,
johnny b. goode, sweet baby,
talkin' 'bout the queen of soul aretha's words,
hey hey hey, hallelujah,
shoutin' inside fabric of gospel, respect,

seven throw eleven wins
the game of dice, seven throw eleven wins

vowels, blind deep singing ray charles,
stevie wonder then took them voice gymnastics

way 'cross town where godfather
of funky soul was gettin' up on the good foot
of rhythmic black language,
while the king of world music moonwalked backwards
up on tippy-toes waving

one sequined glove, hat cocked, breaking syllables
in a million different ways,
all handed down through african cultural
metamorphosis, brought here,
transmogrified now in tongues in sun ra's space
travels, voodoo child jimi
hendrix dropped bombs from his airplane guitar blasts
at woodstock, thrilled history,
whitney houston, living color, cameo
naughty by nature, fugees,
arrested development, a tribe called quest,

seven throw eleven wins
the game of life, seven throw eleven wins

rappers, public enemy,
tupac, biggie, snoop doggie dogg, jay-z, nas,
rapping to the core, j. cole
dr. dre, kanye west, kendrick lamar, bold
all this black power, human,
delivers female power in macy gray,
beyoncé & rihanna,

eye am writing these words sitting at my desk
in my study, overlooking little senegal,

on 116th street, harlem, new york,
eye am thinking of the door of no return in gorée,
eye am thinking of sitting on my veranda one night
when stars were diamonds in an ink-black sky
& waves were foaming in from the sea
with sacred voices back in goyave, guadeloupe,
where the genesis for this poem first rooted,
grew metaphors, bloomed from those seeds into flowers
transformed into words, that grew wings on images
& flew through sentences as birds up in the blue
music of the sky sluicing new voices,

all of this was rooted in mystery, beauty—ugliness too—
after african ghost spirit crabs transformed themselves
into voodoo spirit loas through the spirits of legba, erzulie, agwe
on a beach in haiti, then were reborn in me in guadeloupe
through seduction in my sleep while dreaming,
before being transferred, transmogrified rapture,
rhapsody in the free-flowing structure of this episodic poem
created through african-american hoodoo spirituality,
inhabiting me now here in harlem, as *eye* sit in my study
writing it all down into this living, breathing poem
chronicling a very long, tortuous journey of miracles,
resurrections, the redemptive legacy of blackamoors,
hoping you readers, listeners, are hearing this testimony
now, too, paying attention to all these spirits
speaking in tongues through this poem,

seven throw eleven wins
the game of dice, seven throw eleven wins,

seven throw eleven wins
the game of life, seven throw eleven wins

love, holiness, *FREEDOM, IT,*

seven throw eleven wins
games of life, seven throw eleven wins *IT*